OTTERS SMASH, CRABS PINCH

HUNTER AND HUNTED
ANIMAL SURVIVAL

DOROTHY JENNINGS

PowerKiDS
press.

New York

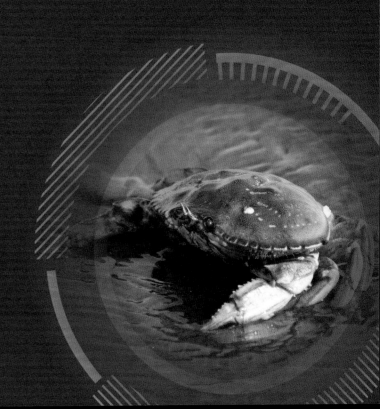

Published in 2018 by The Rosen Publishing Group, Inc.
29 East 21st Street, New York, NY 10010

First Edition

Editor: Theresa Morlock
Book Design: Reann Nye

Photo Credits: Cover (sea otter) belizar/Shutterstock.com; cover (crab), pp. 1, 13, 14 SNC Art and More/Shutterstock.com; p. 4 Helder Gomes/Shutterstock.com; p. 5 pingebat/Shutterstock.com; p. 6 David Litman/Shutterstock.com; p. 7 Chase Dekker/Shutterstock.com; p. 8 Menno Schaefer/Shutterstock.com; p. 9 Tom Soucek/First Light/Getty Images; p. 10 Jean-Edouard Rozey/Shutterstock.com; pp. 11, 21 David Courtenay/Oxford Scientific/Getty Images; p. 12 Glenn Price/Shutterstock.com; p. 15 Krista Kennell/Shutterstock.com; p. 16 clayton harrison/Shutterstock.com; p. 17 tab62/Shutterstock.com; p. 18 Kris Wiktor/Shutterstock.com; p. 19 Angelo DeSantis/Moment Open/Getty Images; p. 20 Greg Amptman/Shutterstock.com; p. 22 (otter) tryton2011/Shutterstock.com; p. 22 (Dungeness crab) Dan Schreiber/Shutterstock.com.

Library of Congress Cataloging-in-Publication Data

Names: Jennings, Dorothy, 1961- author.
Title: Otters smash, crabs pinch / Dorothy Jennings.
Description: New York : PowerKids Press, [2018] | Series: Hunter and hunted :
  animal survival | Includes index.
Identifiers: LCCN 2017005874| ISBN 9781508156697 (pbk. book) | ISBN
  9781508156512 (6 pack) | ISBN 9781508156628 (library bound book)
Subjects: LCSH: Marine animals–Pacific Coast (U.S.)–Juvenile literature.
Classification: LCC QL122.2 .J48 2018 | DDC 591.77–dc23
LC record available at https://lccn.loc.gov/2017005874

Manufactured in the United States of America

CPSIA Compliance Information: Batch Batch #BS17PK: For Further Information contact Rosen Publishing, New York, New York at 1-800-237-9932

CONTENTS

LIFE ON THE PACIFIC COAST

On the Pacific coast of the United States, the chilly water is teeming with life. Clams burrow in the sand, sea stars creep along the ocean floor, and harbor seals sunbathe on the shore. In the distance, orcas and humpback whales swim, while puffins fly overhead.

The Dungeness crab and sea otter are two of the hundreds of **species** living in the coastal waters of the Pacific. They are able to survive cold temperatures and strong **tides**, but can this hunter-and-hunted pair survive each other?

SEA OTTER HABITAT

RUSSIA

ALASKA

CANADA

JAPAN

UNITED STATES

Sea otters can be found in the coastal waters of Alaska, Washington, and California, as well as Canada, Russia, and Japan. Dungeness crabs live on the West Coast of North America.

MARINE MAMMALS

There are 13 different species of otters. The sea otter is the only otter species that gives birth in water. They are one of the smallest marine mammals on the planet. Adults are about 4 feet (1.22 m) long and weigh about 65 pounds (30 kg). As their name suggests, sea otters spend most of their lives in the ocean, in shallow waters along the Pacific coast.

Sea otters have special **adaptations** for sea life. Their feet are webbed for swimming, their nostrils and ears close up to keep out water, and their thick fur is waterproof.

Sea otter mothers float on their back and carry their pups on their chest.

WILDLIFE WISDOM

Unlike other marine animals, sea otters don't have **blubber** to keep them warm. Instead, their **dense** fur blocks out water and locks in heat. A sea otter's coat has 1 million hairs per square inch! That's more than any other animal on Earth.

SEA OTTER BEHAVIORS

Sea otters are very neat creatures. When they aren't eating or sleeping, they're usually cleaning their fur. This is an important task because dirty fur can't keep warmth in as well as clean fur can. Staying clean also helps them stay waterproof.

Sea otters are often seen floating on their back. They sleep this way, sometimes in groups called rafts. To stay in one place, otters will tangle themselves in seaweed or kelp, which keeps them from being pulled away by the tide.

WILDLIFE WISDOM

Sea otters are an endangered species. That means they're at risk of dying out completely. These animals were once targeted by hunters who wished to sell their fur. By the beginning of the 20th century, there were only about 1,000 to 2,000 sea otters left. It's now illegal to hunt sea otters, but they're still at risk.

When sea otters sleep, they sometimes hold each other's paws so that they don't drift apart.

AN OTTER'S FEAST

Sea otters are carnivores, or meat eaters. They eat about a quarter of their body weight in food per day. Sea otters hunt squid, octopuses, fish, sea urchins, and several kinds of crabs, including Dungeness crabs. They can dive as deep as 330 feet (100.6 m) to look for food.

Sea otters eat over 100 different species of sea creatures.

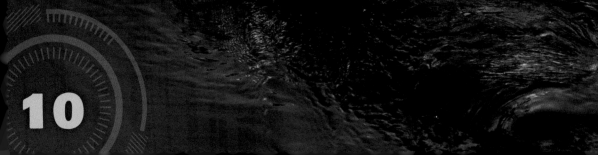

SEA URCHIN

ROCK

Sea otters are some of the only animals known to use tools! They pick up rocks from the ocean floor and carry them in their armpits. When they snatch a hard-to-crack meal like a crab, they smash it against the rock until it breaks open.

11

CRAB BASICS

Dungeness crabs are some of the biggest crabs to live along the Pacific coast of the United States. Males can be 7 to 9 inches (17.8 to 23 cm) wide and 4 to 5 inches (10.2 to 12.7 cm) long. Dungeness crabs are oval shaped with a hard **exoskeleton** called a carapace, or shell. As they grow, a new shell forms underneath this exoskeleton and they molt, or shed, the old one.

Crabs have two pairs of **antennae**, which are used to feel, taste, and smell. They have four pairs of legs for walking, as well as a pair of pincers.

WILDLIFE WISDOM

Crabs have a special ability—they can regrow parts of their body! If a crab loses a leg to a predator, its body can grow a new leg to replace it. Replacement parts can take a long time to grow and may never be as large as the old ones were.

Crabs walk sideways because their legs are attached to the sides of their body. If they walked forward, they'd trip!

13

WHERE'S DUNGENESS?

Dungeness crabs got their name from the town of Dungeness, Washington, which was the first place that people caught and sold the crabs in large amounts.

Dungeness crabs are carnivores. They eat fish, clams, other crabs, and other small sea creatures.

Dungeness crabs **mate** during spring and summer. A female crab can carry up to 2.5 million eggs. The young crabs are able to take care of themselves as soon as they hatch. Young crabs go through several stages of growth. They reach adulthood when they're about three years old. Dungeness crabs can live between 8 and 13 years in the wild.

A CRAB'S LIFE

Dungeness crabs live underwater on sandy ocean bottoms near the shore. They're purplish brown, which helps them blend in with their surroundings. A crab's underside is yellow or cream colored. Crabs bury themselves in sand to avoid predators. When faced with a predator, they may roll onto their back so that they can attack with their pincers.

Dungeness crabs turn orange when they're cooked.

Dungeness crabs have many predators. They're not only hunted by sea otters, but by other crabs, octopuses, fish, and people. People catch crabs in steel traps called pots.

FACE-OFF!

A hungry sea otter dives to the ocean floor in search of a meal. Hidden in the sand, a Dungeness crab keeps still, trying to blend in with its surroundings. The sea otter spots the crab and snatches it up with its paws, carrying it up to the surface of the water.

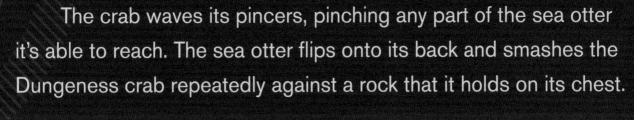

The crab waves its pincers, pinching any part of the sea otter it's able to reach. The sea otter flips onto its back and smashes the Dungeness crab repeatedly against a rock that it holds on its chest.

Will the crab's pincers and hard shell **protect** it from the otter? Or will the sea otter smash the crab and eat it?

19

KEEPING THE BALANCE

Sea otters are a keystone species, which is a species that plays a very important part in its **ecosystem**. If a keystone species is removed from an ecosystem, many other species suffer. An important way that sea otters help their ecosystem is by eating many other species. Without sea otters as a predator, the ecosystem could be overpopulated by prey species.

Although they are predators and prey, sea otters and Dungeness crabs both contribute to their ecosystem. Sea otters help by eating other species and crabs help by cleaning up the ocean floor.

Sea otters live in areas with kelp, or giant seaweed. Urchins eat kelp. Without sea otters to eat the urchins, the kelp might die out.

TEAM OTTER VS. TEAM CRAB

Sea otters usually have the advantage when battling crabs. Sea otters have whiskers, which pick up movements in the water, helping them find hiding crabs. They also have sharp teeth to help them crush a crab's hard exoskeleton. If caught by an otter, a crab's only hope is to pinch it hard enough that the otter will drop it before it can be eaten.

Who would you root for in the battle of life and death? Would it be the smashing sea otter or the pinching crab?

GLOSSARY

adaptation: A change in a living thing that helps it live better in its habitat.

antenna: A feeler on the head of some animals. The plural of "antenna" is "antennae."

blubber: The fat on whales and other large marine mammals.

dense: Closely packed together or thick.

ecosystem: A natural community of living and nonliving things.

exoskeleton: The hard covering on the outside of an animal's body that holds and guards the soft insides.

mate: To come together to make babies.

protect: To keep safe.

species: A group of plants or animals that are all the same kind.

tide: The daily rise and fall of the ocean.

INDEX

WEBSITES

Due to the changing nature of Internet links, PowerKids Press has developed an online list of websites related to the subject of this book. This site is updated regularly. Please use this link to access the list: www.powerkidslinks.com/handh/otter